The Number Team and the Great Race

Sally Hewitt

illustrated by Ruth Rivers

Thameside Press

Notes for parents and teachers
How to use this book

Each double page has a numeracy theme,
such as days of the week, shapes, or position.

The story ——

Question boxes ——

Monkey's
math tip

Question boxes

Each box has two questions. Elephant's questions
are easier than Crocodile's. Start with Elephant's
questions, then move on to Crocodile's. Or you
can choose to answer only Elephant's or only
Crocodile's questions. The answers are on page 30.

 Find the food that is
not fruit.

 Think of different ways
to sort the food.

Monkey's math tip

Read Monkey's math tip for help with
the Number Team's questions, or extra
information about the math in the scene.

There are ideas for games
and activities on page 31.

Sorting and sets

You can sort an object
by describing what it is.
A potato is something to
eat and it has a skin. You
can also sort it by saying
what it is not. A potato is
not a fruit, for example.

Meet the Number Team

Crocodile, Lion, Monkey, and Elephant
are planning their route for the Great Air Race.
They will fly their hot-air balloon over deserts
and mountains, islands and icebergs. But can
they beat their rivals, the Flash Flyers?

If the teams finish the race in 5 days, what day will they get back?

Tell the time story of the Jungle Jets' famous race.

Time stories

Tell your friends time stories about things that happen to you, like this:

I got home from school at half past three and played football until a quarter past four.
I played football for 45 minutes, or three-quarters of an hour.

The teams get ready for the race. "How much food should we take?" wonders Lion.

How many of each kind of food is Lion packing for the race?

If the race takes 5 days, how many loaves, chocolate bars, and melons can the Number Team eat each day?

Dividing

To work out how many loaves the Number Team can have each day, divide 20 loaves by 5 days: $20 \div 5 = 4$

They could eat more loaves on one day than another, to make a calculation like this:
$6 + 4 + 2 + 3 + 5 = 20$

Find all the groups of 5 things to eat.

Count in fives to find how many things to eat there are altogether.

How many more doughnuts than cakes is Rhino packing?

If the race takes 5 days, how many cakes, pies, and doughnuts can the Flash Flyers eat each day?

"Ready, get set, go!" shouts Zebra. The Flash Flyers zoom into the lead as their supporters cheer them on.

Which team is flying slower? How can you tell?

Which team will reach the forest first? Can you say why?

START

Which animals on the ground are moving quickly? Which are moving slowly?

Which animal will reach the big tree first? Guess which will reach it last.

How many seconds have the teams been in the air?

If the Number Team takes 180 seconds to reach the trees, how many times will the second hand go round the clock?

Seconds

There are 60 seconds in one minute. It takes the second hand on a clock one minute to move all the way around once. A digital stopwatch measures time in seconds. You start it and stop it by pressing the button.

`00:10`

In the control tower the team leaders, Crocodile and Rat, follow the race on a map.

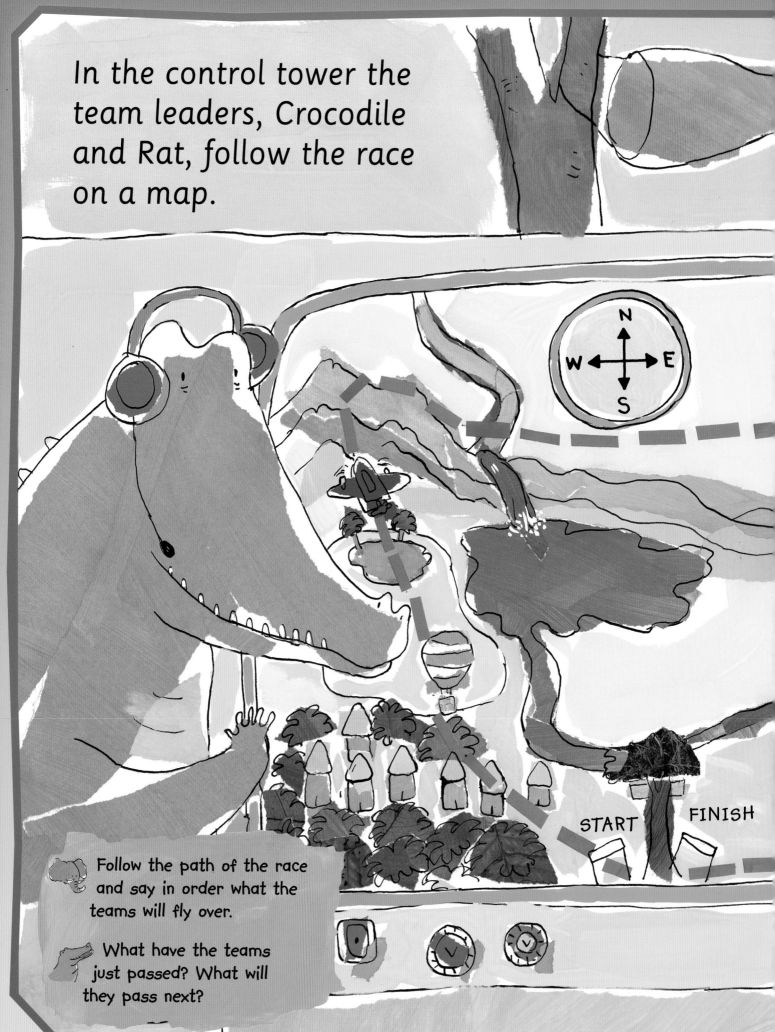

START   FINISH

Follow the path of the race and say in order what the teams will fly over.

What have the teams just passed? What will they pass next?

Find 3 features on the map that are north of the big lake.

Find 5 features on the map that are south of the big lake.

North, south, east, and west

Remember these facts to help you to find your direction:

The sun rises in the east. It shines in the south at midday. It sets in the west. It never shines in the north.

Be careful never to look directly at the sun!

Is the sea east or west of the mountains?

What feature on the map is the farthest east?

The Flash Flyers fly into the trees. The Number Team floats by into the lead.

Tell a number story in words about the giraffes eating and drinking.

The calculation 7 + 4 = 11 tells the story of the giraffes. Find a different calculation to tell the story.

Make a calculation about the zebras using numbers and the + sign.

Find which animals the calculation 10 − 6 = 4 is a number story about.

Calculations

You make a calculation when you work out a number problem. There are four operations: addition, subtraction, multiplication, and division.
Each operation has a symbol or sign.

+ add   − take away or subtract
× multiply ÷ divide

Fourteen animals were asleep, but eight woke up and ran off, leaving six. Find this story in the picture.

Tell number stories from the picture in as many different ways as you can.

"Fly over the mountains,"
says Crocodile.
"Go through the valleys,"
Rat tells her team.

Which mountains are higher than the one with the trees?

Find 3 mountains you would describe as high, higher, and highest.

Which object should Lion or Elephant drop to make the balloon as light as possible?

Estimate which of the objects held by Elephant and Lion is the lightest. Try to put their objects in order of weight. Start with the lightest.

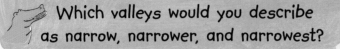 Only one valley is wide enough
for the Flash Flyers to fly through.
Which is it? Which valleys are too narrow?

Which valleys would you describe
as narrow, narrower, and narrowest?

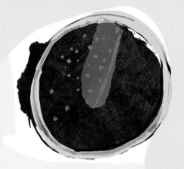

Estimating weight

You can usually compare the height,
width, or length of things just by looking
at them. It's much harder to tell if things
are light or heavy. You will need to pick
them up or weigh them to find out.

Beyond the mountains the weather is wintry. The teams land in the snow for some fun.

Are Monkey's snowball and Lion's snowman both symmetrical shapes?

Can you find more than 1 line of symmetry on Monkey's snowball?

Symmetry

A shape is symmetrical if it has 2 halves that look exactly the same.

A line of symmetry cuts a shape into 2 identical halves. Try putting a mirror along the line of symmetry of a circle. What do you see?

Are both the balloon and the Flash Flyer symmetrical shapes?

Where are the lines of symmetry on Hyena's snowman and the igloo?

How many things can you see in the picture that have a symmetrical shape?

Which shapes can you see that are not symmetrical?

17

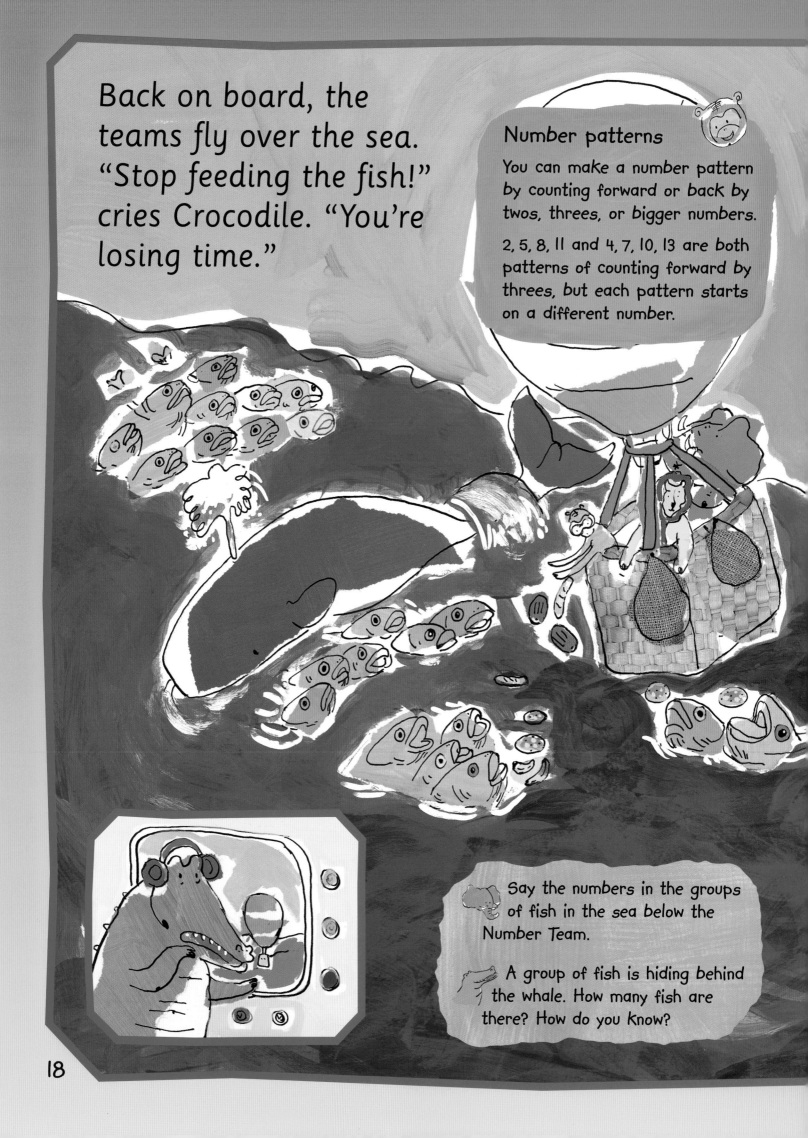

Back on board, the teams fly over the sea. "Stop feeding the fish!" cries Crocodile. "You're losing time."

Number patterns

You can make a number pattern by counting forward or back by twos, threes, or bigger numbers.

2, 5, 8, 11 and 4, 7, 10, 13 are both patterns of counting forward by threes, but each pattern starts on a different number.

Say the numbers in the groups of fish in the sea below the Number Team.

A group of fish is hiding behind the whale. How many fish are there? How do you know?

Find a number pattern in the groups of seagulls.

A group of seagulls is hiding behind the Flash Flyer. How many seagulls are there? How do you know?

How many dolphins have dived under the waves?

Look at the number pattern made by the 3 groups of dolphins. How many dolphins could be in the next 3 groups. How do you know?

A storm brews and the teams take shelter on a desert island. The wind howls and the waves crash.

Find straight lines and curved lines in the picture.

Find 2 different flat shapes with curved lines, and 2 different flat shapes with straight lines.

Find solid shapes with curved surfaces.

Find a solid shape with curved surfaces and flat faces.

Find half-hidden shapes in the sky, the sand, and the sea. What shapes are they?

How many hollow shapes can you find?

Curved surfaces

Spheres, cones, and cylinders are all solid shapes with curved surfaces.

sphere   cone   cylinder

Spheres have no flat faces. Cones stand on a flat circular face. Cylinders have flat circular faces at each end.

21

The next morning, the Flash Flyers take off first. "Look what you left behind!" laughs Monkey.

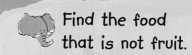 Find the food that is not fruit.

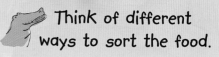 Think of different ways to sort the food.

Find the equipment used for sleeping.

Think of different ways of sorting the equipment.

22

Find the equipment and food that does not belong to the Number Team.

Find the equipment that does not belong to the Flash Flyers and is not used for sleeping.

Sorting and sets

You can sort an object by describing what it is. A potato is something to eat and it has a skin. You can also sort it by saying what it is not. A potato is not a fruit, for example.

The teams are neck and neck on the last leg of the race. "Watch out for the bridge!" yells Rat.

Did Crocodile or Rat tell their team to fly lower?

What instructions did Crocodile give his team to miss the bridge?

Just before
the finishing line
the Number Team
sweeps into the lead.

Which is the biggest group
of animals on the ground?
Which is the smallest?

Put the groups of animals
in order. Start with the
smallest group.

Which group of animals is the same number as the giraffes?

Which groups of animals are bigger than the group of turtles?

Which group of animals is nearest the finish? Which is farthest away?

Which groups of animals are second, third, fourth, and fifth nearest to the finish?

Groups

Numbers can be bigger or smaller than each other, or they can be the same.

20 is a bigger number than 15.
3 is a smaller number than 7.
6 and 6 are the same.

An elephant is bigger than a mouse, but 3 mice make a bigger group than 2 elephants. A group of 2 mice and a group of 2 elephants are the same because there is the same number in each group.

At the Great Air Race party, Monkey holds the cup high. Everyone joins in the celebrations.

The Number Team

Winners of the Great Air Race

4 days, 23 hours, and 30 minutes

Has the Number Team broken the Jungle Jets' record of 5 days?

Look at the poster on page 4. How much faster were the Number Team than the Jungle Jets?

Estimate how many animals are in different groups. Count and check to see if you were right.

Pick 4 groups. Quickly add the numbers of animals together. Check to see if you were right.

Make up a number story about the monkeys playing on the 2 aircraft.

Make up number stories about things going on in the picture.

Days, hours, and minutes

You will need to know that there are 24 hours in a day and 60 minutes in an hour to find out if the Number Team has broken the Jungle Jets' record of 5 days.

29

Answers

Elephant and Crocodile ask both open and closed questions. Closed questions have just one correct answer. Open questions have a number of different correct answers. These will encourage your child to think of alternative answers and, in some cases, to count all the different possibilities.

4–5 Days of the week

- It is Sunday today.
- The Jungle Jets started on Tuesday.

- They would get back on Thursday.
- They would get back on Saturday.

- They will get back on Friday.
- The Jungle Jets set off on Tuesday. They crossed the finish line on Saturday. They took 5 days to finish the race.

6–7 Calculations

- 20 loaves of bread, 10 chocolate bars, 5 melons.
- 4 loaves, 2 chocolate bars, and 1 melon each day.

- Loaves of bread, chocolate bars, melons, doughnuts, pies, and cakes.
- 65 things to eat (20 loaves, 10 chocolate bars, 5 melons, 15 doughnuts, 10 pies, and 5 cakes).

- 10 more doughnuts.
- 3 doughnuts, 2 pies, and 1 cake each day.

8–9 Fast and slow

- The Number Team is slower. You can tell because they are closest to the start line.
- The Flash Flyers will probably reach the forest first, because they are flying faster so far.

- Quickly: the supporters of the Flash Flyers (the cheetah, monkey, turtle, giraffe, hippo, and wildebeest beneath the Flash Flyer). Slowly: the supporters of the Number Team (the giraffe, wildebeest, cheetah, turtle, and hippo on the left-hand page).
- First: the cheetah ahead of the Flash Flyer. Last: the old hippo by the start line.

- 10 seconds.
- 3 times round the clock.

10–11 North, south, east, west

- A village, a pool, mountains, a river, the coast, icebergs, an island, the coast, a jungle, a river.
- The Flash Flyers have just passed a pool and will pass the mountains next. The balloon has just passed the village and will pass the pool next.

- North: Flash Flyer, mountains, waterfall, icebergs, dolphins, lighthouse, island.
- South: balloon, jungle, village, river, delta, control tower, start and finish lines.

- The sea is east of the mountains.
- The lighthouse is farthest east.

12–13 Number stories

- Seven giraffes are eating and four giraffes are drinking. That makes eleven altogether.
- 11 − 7 = 4. (Eleven giraffes were drinking at the pool. Seven went off to eat, leaving four.)

- 9 + 5 + 2 = 16.
- The wildebeest. (Ten were on the far side of the river. Six crossed over, leaving four).

- This is a story about the deer.
- One story is: sixteen zebras were drinking at the pool. Two went to sleep under a tree. Nine went off to graze, leaving five by the pool.

14–15 Comparing measurements

- The brown mountain and the snowy mountain.
- High: mountain with trees. Higher: brown mountain. Highest: snowy mountain.

- Elephant should drop the sandbag, because it is heaviest.
- The banana is lightest, then the spanner, then the melon. The sandbag is the heaviest.

- Wide enough: the valley farthest to the right. Too narrow: the valley on the left and the 2 valleys in the middle.
- Narrow: the second valley from the left. Narrower: the third valley from the left. Narrowest: the valley farthest to the left.

16–17 Symmetry

- Yes, they are both symmetrical.
- Any line that passes through the center of the snowball is a line of symmetry. That means there is an infinite number of lines of symmetry.

- Yes, both the Flash Flyer and the balloon are symmetrical.
- Straight down the middle, from top to bottom.

- Symmetrical: the igloo, Lion's snowman, the balloon, the Flash Flyer, Hyena's snowman, and the penguin to the left of Hyena.
- Not symmetrical: the polar bears, the fish, the seals, Monkey, Lion, Elephant, Rhino, Hyena, and many more.

18–19 Number patterns

- 10, 6, 4, and 2 fish.
- 8 fish (to complete the sequence of counting down in twos).

- 3, 6, and 12 seagulls (doubling each time).
- 9 seagulls are hiding (to make a sequence of counting backward by threes: 3, 6, 9, 12).

- 5 dolphins have dived under the waves.
- It could be 7, 9, and 11 dolphins (carrying on the sequence of counting forward by twos), or 1, 3, and 5 dolphins (repeating the sequence).

20–21 Shapes

- Straight lines: the edges of the Number Team's tent, the taut ropes, and many more. Curved lines: the circles, spirals, and wavy lines on the Number Team's tent, and many more.
- Flat shapes with curved lines: circles and spirals on the Number Team's tent. Flat shapes with straight lines: squares and triangles on the Flash Flyers' tent.

- The rolled-up mats and the oil drum (cylinders); Elephant's ball of balloon canvas (sphere); sea shells (cones); sandbags (ovoids).
- A cylinder (the rolled-up mats and the oil drum).

- The moon in the sky (sphere); shells in the sand (cones); oil drums in the sea (cylinders).
- The tents, the empty boxes, the balloon basket, and the tree trunk by the Flash Flyer.

22–23 Sorting and sets

- Not fruit: loaves of bread, chocolate bars, cakes, pies, and doughnuts.
- Whether it has been cooked (bread, cakes, pies, doughnuts); whether it has a skin (all the fruit).

- Tents, sleeping bags, blankets, cushions.
- Tools (spanners, hammers, screwdrivers); whether it can be rolled up (blankets, sleeping bags, tents), for example.

- Everything on the right-hand page: spanner, screwdriver, hammer, oil cans, cakes, pies, pineapples, bananas, doughnuts, and oranges.
- Life belt, ropes, sandbags, balloon, hammer, water bottles, screwdrivers, and spanners (all on the left-hand page).

24–25 Position

- Rat told her team to fly lower.
- Crocodile said "Fly higher, over the bridge!"

- Crocodile warned "Watch out, behind you!"
- Above a flock of birds, behind the Number Team, below an eagle.

- Crocodile and Rat in the control tower.
- Left: the Flash Flyers. Right: the Number Team.

26–27 Groups of numbers

- Biggest: cheetahs (6). Smallest: wildebeest (2).
- Wildebeest (2), hippos and giraffes (3), turtles (4), monkeys (5), cheetahs (6).

- Nearest: monkeys. Farthest away: hippos.
- 2nd: giraffes. 3rd: wildebeest. 4th: cheetahs. 5th: turtles.

- There are the same number of hippos (3).
- The monkeys (5) and the cheetahs (6).

28–29 Time and numbers

- Yes, the Number Team have broken the record.
- The Number Team was 30 minutes faster.

- For example, there are 6 monkeys in the balloon, 3 monkeys in the Flash Flyer, 6 animals in the orchestra, and 3 cheetahs dancing in a circle.
- For example: add the number of animals in the orchestra, the monkeys in the balloon, the cheetahs in a line, and the turtles on each other's shoulders to make 18 (6 + 6 + 3 + 3 = 18).

- Three monkeys are in the Flash Flyer, and six are playing in the balloon, making nine altogether.
- For example: fourteen melons were on the table, but eight rolled off, leaving six. Three cheetahs are dancing in a line, and three are dancing in a circle, making six altogether.

Notes for parents and teachers
Games and activities

Use the Number Team's questions to help you find more math in the pictures. Then try these games and activities:

4–5 Calendars

Use a calendar to have a quiz, with questions such as:
- April 20 is a Friday. What day of the week is April 24?
- How many days are there in September?
- May 1 is a Thursday. What day of the week is April 29?

6–7 Counting in fives

Plan 5 packed lunches for Monday to Friday. If you make lunches for 5 children each day, how many lunches are there altogether? Make a shopping list of the food for all the lunches.

8–9 Seconds and minutes

Time how long it takes to eat breakfast. Use a calculator to work out how many seconds it took. If it took 15 minutes, the calculation is 15 x 60. How many seconds a week do you spend eating breakfast? How many traveling to school?

14–15 Weight

Make cookies. Heat the oven to 320°F. Weigh out 7 oz of butter, 7 oz of sugar and 10 oz of flour. Beat the butter and sugar, add an egg, and mix in the flour. Make the dough into 40 balls and flatten them onto a greased baking sheet. Cook for 15 minutes.

16–17 Symmetry

Fold a piece of paper in half, then open it flat. With thick paints, paint a pattern on one side up to but not over the fold line. While the paint is wet, fold the paper again and press gently. Open it out to find a symmetrical pattern.

18–19 Number patterns

Make up number patterns using 4 numbers: 20, 16, 12, 8, for example. Write the numbers on separate cards and lay them out in order. Turn one card over. Who can work out the missing number?

20–21 Straight and curved lines

Take a pencil for a walk, drawing only curved lines. Now do the same on another sheet of paper, drawing only straight lines. Color in the spaces between the lines. What can you say about the shapes of these spaces?

24–25 Left and right

Give very fast instructions to your friends, such as—stand on your left leg, wave your right hand, shut your left eye. Whoever gets left and right mixed up is given a penalty point. Three penalty points and you're out!

Distributed in the United States by
Smart Apple Media
1980 Lookout Drive
North Mankato, MN 56003

Text by Sally Hewitt
Illustrations by Ruth Rivers

Series editor: Mary-Jane Wilkins
Editor: Russell McLean
Designer: John Jamieson
Educational consultant: Katie Kitching, Buckland
    Infants School, Chessington, Surrey, U.K.

ISBN 1-930643-66-7

Library of Congress Control Number: 2001088844

Printed in China

9 8 7 6 5 4 3 2 1

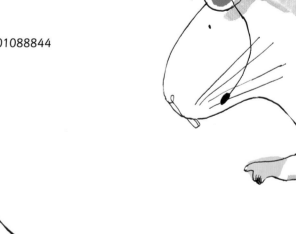

DATE DUE

DEC 20 '01			
JAN 31 '02			
FEB 13 '02			
APR 25 '02			

DEMCO 38-296